OVERBEARING PARENTS:

What causes parental control and what we can do about it

Dustin P. Robert

Table of Contents

Chapter 1:

Introduction

What is "forbearing parents"?

As a young girl, Sarah always knew her mother meant well. She wanted nothing more than to protect her daughter from the hardships of the world and ensure that she had every opportunity to succeed. But as Sarah grew older, she began to feel suffocated by her mother's constant hovering and overbearing control. From what clothes she wore to who she hung out with, everything seemed to be dictated by her mother's wishes.

Sarah's mother meant well, but her excessive control was stifling her daughter's growth and independence. Sarah struggled to make her own decisions and find her own way in the world, always feeling like she had to live up to her mother's expectations. It wasn't until Sarah left for college that she was able to break free of her mother's controlling influence and start building her own identity.

Sarah's story is not uncommon. Many parents struggle with the balance between nurturing and overbearing, trying to find the sweet spot where they can protect and guide their children without stifling their growth and development.

Forbearing parents are those who exercise a high level of control over their children's lives, often to the point of interfering with their autonomy and independence. This type of parenting style is characterized by a lack of trust in the child's ability to make decisions and handle challenges on their own.

As a result, the parent takes on a more authoritarian role, dictating what the child should do and think.

While all parents naturally want to protect and guide their children, excessive control can have negative consequences for the child's development and well-being. It can hinder their ability to learn and grow, and may even contribute to mental health issues such as anxiety and low self-esteem.

In this book, we will delve into the causes of excessive parental control and provide strategies for overcoming it. By understanding the importance of a healthy balance in parenting, we can help our children grow into confident, capable adults. We will examine the effects of this parenting style on children and discuss how to find a balance between nurturing and overbearing. By the end of this book, you will have a better understanding of the importance of parental control and how to implement positive parenting techniques.

Chapter 2:

The Importance of Parental Control

As a parent, one of your most important roles is shaping your child's development and helping them become independent, responsible adults. While it may be tempting to try and control every aspect of your child's life in order to keep them safe and ensure their success, it is important to find a balance between nurturing and overbearing.

Parental control refers to the boundaries and expectations you set for your child as they grow and learn. These can include rules for behavior, decision-making, and responsibilities. By setting appropriate limits and boundaries, you can help your child learn self-control and develop a sense of responsibility.

However, excessive parental control can have negative consequences for your child's development. It can hinder their ability to learn and grow, and may even contribute to mental health issues such as anxiety and low self-esteem. When children are not given the opportunity to make their own decisions and solve problems on their own, they may struggle with independence and decision-making later in life.

On the other hand, a lack of parental control can also be harmful to a child's development. Without boundaries and guidance, children may struggle to understand appropriate behavior and may engage in risky or harmful activities.

Finding a balance between nurturing and overbearing is key to supporting your child's development. It is important to set limits and expectations for your child, but also to allow them the freedom to make their own mistakes and learn from them. By striking this balance, you can help your child become a confident, capable adult.

The role of parents in shaping a child's development

As a parent, your influence on your child's development is immense. From the moment your child is born, you play a crucial role in shaping their personality, values, and behaviors. How you interact with your child and the environment you provide for them can have a lasting impact on their development.

Consider the case of Jake and his parents. Jake's parents were both highly successful professionals who placed a strong emphasis on education and career advancement. From a young age, Jake's parents set high expectations for his performance in school and extracurricular activities. They provided him with all the resources he needed to excel, including private tutors, enrichment programs, and study materials. Jake's parents were always there to support him and encourage him to strive for excellence.

As a result of his parents' influence, Jake grew up to be a highly motivated and successful young man. He excelled in school, received numerous awards and accolades, and went on to attend a prestigious university. Jake's parents were proud of their son's achievements and felt that their efforts had paid off.

However, Jake's parents' constant focus on his performance and success had a downside. Jake always felt pressure to succeed and lived in fear of disappointing his parents. He struggled with anxiety and perfectionism, and often felt overwhelmed by the demands placed on him. Despite his successes, Jake sometimes wished that his parents had given him more freedom to explore his own interests and passions, rather than always pushing him to excel.

Jake's story illustrates the powerful influence that parents can have on their children's development. While setting high expectations and providing support can help children achieve success, it is important to find a balance between nurturing and overbearing. It is essential to allow children the freedom to explore their own interests and make their own decisions, rather than constantly directing their path. By finding this balance, parents can help their children grow into confident, capable adults.

The benefits of setting boundaries and expectations

As a parent, it can be difficult to strike the right balance between nurturing and overbearing. You want to protect your child and ensure their safety and success, but you also don't want to stifle their growth and independence. One way to find this balance is through the use of boundaries and expectations.

Boundaries are limits that you set for your child in order to help them understand appropriate behavior and keep them safe. These can include rules for things like bedtimes, screen time, and behavior in public. Expectations are the standards you set for your child's behavior and responsibilities. These can include things like completing homework, helping with household chores, and following rules.

Setting boundaries and expectations can have numerous benefits for your child's development. These can include:

- Improved self-control: By setting boundaries and expectations, you can help your child learn self-control and make responsible decisions.
- Increased independence: When children are given the opportunity to make their own choices within the limits set by their parents, they can learn to be more independent and responsible.
- Enhanced problem-solving skills: When children are faced with challenges and expectations, they must learn to think critically and come up with solutions. This helps them develop problem-solving skills that will serve them well throughout their lives.

For example, consider the case of Jenny, a nine-year-old who always struggled with bedtimes. Her parents had always had a strict bedtime routine, but Jenny would often try to push the limits and stay up later. Frustrated with her daughter's disobedience, Jenny's mother decided to set a new boundary. She told Jenny that she could choose her own bedtime, as long as she was in bed and asleep by 8:00 p.m. At first, Jenny was thrilled with this new freedom and stayed up later than usual. But after a few days of feeling tired and cranky, she realized that she needed a full night's sleep in order to feel rested and ready for the next day. Jenny learned to set her own bedtime and take responsibility for her own sleep. This newfound sense of independence and responsibility helped Jenny grow and develop in ways that strict bedtimes never could have.

By setting appropriate boundaries and expectations, you can help your child develop self-control, independence, and problem-solving skills. These are important life skills that will serve your child well throughout their lives.

The importance of finding a balance in parenting style

As a parent, it can be challenging to find the right balance between nurturing and overbearing. On one hand, you want to protect and guide your child, providing them with the resources and support they need to succeed. On the other hand, you don't want to stifle their growth and independence by being too controlling. Striking this balance is crucial to your child's development and well-being.

One way to find this balance is to consider the different parenting styles and how they can affect your child. Authoritative parenting, for example, involves setting clear boundaries and expectations while also allowing children the freedom to make their own decisions and solve problems on their own. This style has been shown to be the most effective in promoting children's independence and success.

On the other hand, authoritarian parenting involves strict rules and a lack of autonomy for the child. This style can lead to lower self-esteem and poorer social skills in children. Similarly, permissive parenting, which involves little structure or boundaries, can also be harmful to children's development.

It is important to find a balance that works for you and your family. This may involve taking the best aspects of different parenting styles and adapting them to your own situation. It is okay to make mistakes and adjust your approach as you go along. The most important thing is to be mindful of your child's needs and adjust your parenting style accordingly.

By finding a balance in your parenting style, you can support your child's development and help them grow into confident, capable adults.

Examples of healthy and unhealthy levels of parental control

As a parent, it can be difficult to know where the line is between nurturing and overbearing. To better understand the balance between healthy and unhealthy levels of parental control, let's consider a few examples.

Example 1: Healthy parental control

Anna's parents were always there for her, but they also gave her the freedom to explore her own interests and make her own decisions. They set clear boundaries and expectations for her behavior, but also encouraged her to think for herself and solve problems on her own. As a result, Anna grew up to be a confident and independent young woman.

Example 2: Unhealthy parental control

Bob's parents were very controlling and always dictated what he should do and think. They micromanaged every aspect of his life, from his schoolwork to his friendships. Bob never felt like he had the freedom to make his own decisions or explore his own interests. As a result, he struggled with low self-esteem and felt helpless and dependent on his parents.

Example 3: Healthy parental control

Carla's parents were loving and supportive, but they also set clear boundaries and expectations for her behavior. They provided her with the resources and guidance she needed to succeed, but also encouraged her to be independent and make her own decisions. As a result, Carla grew up to be a responsible and confident young woman.

Example 4: Unhealthy parental control

David's parents were extremely controlling and never allowed him to make his own decisions or explore his own interests. They dictated every aspect of his life and punished him severely for any missteps. As a result, David struggled with low self-esteem and felt anxious and helpless.

These examples illustrate the importance of finding a balance in parental control. Too much control can be harmful to a child's development, while too little control can also be detrimental. It is important to set boundaries and expectations for your child, but also to allow them the freedom to make their own decisions and explore their own interests. By finding this balance, you can help your child grow into a confident and capable adult.

Chapter 3:

Causes of Excessive Parental Control

Excessive parental control is often driven by a variety of factors, including parental anxiety or insecurity, past experiences with authority figures, cultural or societal expectations, and family dynamics. Let's examine each of these causes in more detail.

Cause 1: Parental anxiety or insecurity

For some parents, excessive control may stem from feelings of anxiety or insecurity about their child's safety and well-being. These parents may feel the need to constantly monitor and protect their child, believing that they are the only ones who can ensure their child's success and happiness. This type of overbearing behavior can be driven by a variety of underlying fears, such as fear of failure, fear of the unknown, or fear of danger.

Consider the case of Emily and her mother. Emily's mother was always very anxious about her daughter's safety and well-being. She worried constantly about Emily's grades, her friends, and her future. As a result, Emily's mother was always hovering and making decisions for her daughter, never giving her the chance to explore and make her own mistakes. Emily often felt suffocated and resentful of her mother's constant interference.

Emily's mother's anxiety was driven by a variety of underlying fears. She was afraid that Emily would fail or make poor decisions that would jeopardize her future. She was also afraid of the unknown and wanted to protect her daughter from any potential dangers or setbacks. However, her constant control and interference were actually hindering Emily's development and independence. Emily struggled to find her own voice and make the best decisions as her mates.

Cause 2: Past experiences with authority figures

For some parents, excessive control may be a result of past experiences with authority figures. For example, a parent who grew up with strict, authoritarian parents may carry that parenting style into their own parenting. Similarly, a parent who experienced abuse or neglect as a child may be more overprotective of their own children as a result.

Consider the case of Sarah and her daughter, Jessica. Sarah grew up with strict, authoritarian parents who never allowed her to make her own decisions or explore her own interests. They dictated every aspect of her life and punished her severely for any missteps. As a result, Sarah struggled with low self-esteem and felt anxious and helpless.

When Sarah became a parent herself, she vowed to be different. She wanted to give her daughter the freedom and autonomy that she never had. However, Sarah found it difficult to let go of her own controlling tendencies. She struggled to trust Jessica to make her own decisions and often found herself micromanaging every aspect of her daughter's life.

Sarah's past experiences with authoritarian parents had a lasting impact on her own parenting style. It was only through therapy and self-reflection that Sarah was able to recognize the damaging effects of her controlling behavior and learn to let go. By working through her past experiences and finding a balance in her parenting style, Sarah was able to support her daughter's growth and independence.

This example illustrates how past experiences with authority figures can shape a person's parenting style and how it is important to be mindful of these influences in order to find a healthy balance.

Cause 3: Cultural or societal expectations

Cultural and societal expectations can also play a role in excessive parental control. In some cultures, it is expected that parents will be highly involved in their children's lives and make decisions for them. This can lead to a more controlling parenting style.

Consider the case of John and his son, Peter. John was a first-generation immigrant from a traditional Asian culture where parents were expected to play a central role in their children's lives. John's parents had always been very involved in his own upbringing, making all of his decisions for him and dictating his path in life.

When John became a parent himself, he felt pressure to follow the same model. He wanted to ensure that his son had all the opportunities and advantages that he never had. John was highly involved in Peter's schooling and extracurricular activities, always pushing him to excel and succeed.

While John's intentions were good, his controlling behavior began to take a toll on Peter. Peter struggled with low self-esteem and felt like he could never live up to his father's expectations. He never had the opportunity to explore his own interests or make his own decisions.

John eventually realized the damaging effects of his controlling behavior and worked to find a balance between his own cultural expectations and his son's need for independence. By letting go of some control and allowing

Peter to make his own decisions, John was able to support his son's growth and development.

This example illustrates how cultural and societal expectations can influence parenting style and how it is important to be mindful of these influences in order to find a healthy balance.

Cause 4: The role of family dynamics and parenting models

Finally, family dynamics and parenting models can also influence the level of parental control. For example, a family with an authoritarian parenting model may be more prone to excessive control, while a family with a more democratic parenting model may be more balanced and supportive of a child's autonomy.

Family dynamics can also play a role in the level of parental control. For example, a family with a highly hierarchical power structure may be more prone to excessive control, while a family with more equal power dynamics may be more balanced.

It is important to be aware of the influence of family dynamics and parenting models on your own parenting style and to strive to find a balance that works for your family. This may involve adapting elements of different parenting models or seeking out resources and support to help you find the right balance. By finding this balance, you can support your child's development and help them grow into confident, capable adults.

Chapter 4:

The Effects of Excessive Parental Control on Children

Excessive parental control can have a range of negative effects on children. It can hinder their development, impair their emotional well-being, and undermine their confidence and independence. In this chapter, we will examine some of the specific ways in which excessive parental control can impact children, including lack of autonomy and independence, difficulty with decision-making and problem-solving, and negative impacts on mental health and self-esteem. We will also consider examples and case studies of the consequences of excessive parental control.

Effect 1: Lack of autonomy and independence

One of the most significant effects of excessive parental control is the lack of autonomy and independence it can create in children. When parents constantly monitor and direct their children's actions, children may be deprived of the opportunity to make their own decisions and learn from their own experiences. This can inhibit the development of important skills such as problem-solving, decision-making, and critical thinking.

Effect 2: Difficulty with decision-making and problem-solving

Children who are constantly told what to do and think may struggle to develop their own decision-making and problem-solving skills. They may become reliant on their parents to make decisions for them and may be unable to solve problems on their own. This can lead to a lack of self-confidence and an inability to function independently.

Effect 3: Negative impact on mental health and self-esteem

Excessive parental control can also have a negative impact on children's mental health and self-esteem. Children who feel constantly monitored and controlled may struggle with low self-esteem and feelings of inadequacy. They may also feel anxious and depressed as they are unable to explore their own interests or make their own decisions.

Examples and case studies of the consequences of excessive parental control

To better understand the effects of excessive parental control on children, let's consider a few examples and case studies.

Example 1: Sarah and her daughter, Jessica

Sarah grew up with strict, authoritarian parents who never allowed her to make her own decisions or explore her own interests. When Sarah became a parent herself, she struggled to let go of her own controlling tendencies and found it difficult to trust her daughter to make her own decisions. As a result, Jessica struggled with low self-esteem and felt like she could never live up to her mother's expectations.

Example 2: John and his son, Peter

John was a first-generation immigrant from a traditional Asian culture where parents were expected to be highly involved in their children's lives. John was highly involved in his son's schooling and extracurricular activities, always pushing him to excel and succeed. However, this controlling behavior took a toll on Peter's confidence and independence. Peter struggled with low self-esteem and felt like he could never live up to

It is important to recognize the negative effects of excessive parental control and strive to find a balance that supports children's development and well-being. By setting boundaries and expectations while also allowing children the freedom to make their own decisions and explore their own interests, parents can help their children grow into confident, capable adults.

Chapter 5:

Strategies for Overcoming Excessive Parental Control

If you are a parent who struggles with excessive control, it can be challenging to break this pattern and find a more balanced approach to parenting. However, there are several strategies that can help you overcome excessive control and support your child's growth and development. These strategies include communication and setting boundaries, encouraging independence and responsibility, seeking support from trusted sources, and implementing positive parenting techniques.

Strategy 1: Communication and setting boundaries

Effective communication and setting clear boundaries are key to finding a balance in parenting. By setting boundaries, you can establish expectations for your child's behavior and give them the freedom to make their own decisions within those boundaries. At the same time, it is important to have open, honest communication with your child and listen to their perspective. This can help you understand their needs and concerns and find a parenting style that works for both of you.

Here are a few tips for communication and setting boundaries:

a.   Be specific and consistent

It is important to be specific and consistent when setting boundaries. This means clearly stating what is and is not acceptable behavior and consistently enforcing those boundaries. This can help your child understand what is expected of them and feel more secure and supported.

b.   Involve your child in the process

Involve your child in the process of setting boundaries. This can help them feel more invested in following the rules and more aware of their own behavior. You can ask your child for their input, listen to their perspective, and work together to find mutually agreed upon boundaries.

c.   Practice open, honest communication

Open, honest communication is key to effective boundary setting. This means listening to your child's perspective, expressing your own thoughts and feelings, and finding a way to compromise and work together. By having regular, open communication with your child, you can build a strong, supportive relationship and better understand their needs and concerns.

d.   Be flexible and open to negotiation

While it is important to have clear boundaries, it is also important to be flexible and open to negotiation. This means being willing to adapt and adjust boundaries as your child grows and changes and being open to compromise when appropriate.

By using effective communication and setting clear boundaries, you can provide structure and guidance for your child while also supporting their independence and autonomy.

Strategy 2: Encouraging independence and responsibility

Another important strategy for overcoming excessive control is to encourage independence and responsibility in your child. By giving your child the freedom to make their own decisions and take on age-appropriate responsibilities, you can help them develop important life skills and a sense of self-reliance. At the same time, it is important to provide guidance and support as needed and be available to help when problems arise.

Here are a few tips for encouraging independence and responsibility:

i) Start small and gradually increase responsibilities

To encourage independence and responsibility, it is important to start small and gradually increase responsibilities as your child becomes ready. This can involve tasks such as dressing themselves, brushing their own teeth, or helping with household chores. As your child becomes more comfortable and capable, you can gradually increase the level of responsibility.

ii) Encourage problem-solving skills

Encourage your child to use problem-solving skills to find solutions on their own. This can involve asking open-ended questions, brainstorming ideas together, or encouraging your child to think critically and come up with their own solutions. By developing problem-solving skills, your child can become more self-reliant and capable.

iii) Encourage decision-making skills

Encourage your child to make age-appropriate decisions on their own. This can involve allowing them to choose their own clothes, select their own after-school activities, or make simple decisions about their daily routine. By encouraging decision-making skills, you can help your child become more independent and confident.

iv) Provide guidance and support as needed

While it is important to encourage independence and responsibility, it is also important to provide guidance and support as needed. Be available to help when problems arise and offer guidance and support as your child navigates new challenges.

By encouraging independence and responsibility, you can help your child develop important life skills and a sense of self-reliance.

Strategy 3: Seeking support from trusted sources

Parenting can be challenging at times, and it is important to have support from trusted sources. This can involve seeking advice from friends, family, or professionals, such as therapists or parenting experts. By seeking support from trusted sources, you can gain valuable perspective, find new strategies for managing challenges, and feel more supported and equipped as a parent.

Here are a few tips for seeking support from trusted sources:

- Seek out trusted friends and family members

Friends and family members can be a valuable source of support and advice. They can offer a fresh perspective, provide emotional support, and share their own experiences and wisdom. By seeking out trusted friends and family members, you can feel more supported and find new strategies for managing challenges.

- Consider seeking professional support

If you are struggling with excessive parental control or other parenting challenges, it can be helpful to seek professional support. This can involve working with a therapist or seeking advice from a parenting expert. By working with a professional, you can gain valuable insight, find new strategies for managing challenges, and receive support and guidance in a confidential setting.

- Join a parenting group or support group

Joining a parenting group or support group can be a helpful way to find support and advice from others who are facing similar challenges. These groups can provide a sense of community, a place to share experiences and ask questions, and a source of new ideas and strategies.

By seeking support from trusted sources, you can gain valuable perspective, find new strategies for managing challenges, and feel more supported and equipped as a parent.

Tips for implementing positive parenting techniques

Positive parenting is a style of parenting that focuses on building a strong, supportive relationship with your child while setting clear boundaries and expectations. It involves using positive reinforcement, problem-solving skills, and open, honest communication to support your child's development and well-being. Here are a few tips for implementing positive parenting techniques:

1. Use positive reinforcement

Positive reinforcement is a key aspect of positive parenting. It involves reinforcing and praising your child for good behavior and effort. This can help your child feel valued and encourage them to continue exhibiting positive behavior.

Here are a few tips for using positive reinforcement:

i) Offer specific, sincere praise

To be effective, praise should be specific and sincere. Rather than just saying "good job," try to be specific about what you are praising your child for. For example, "I really appreciate how you cleaned up your toys without being asked. That was very responsible of you." This specific, sincere praise can be more meaningful and motivating for your child.

ii) Use rewards appropriately

Rewards can be a helpful way to reinforce positive behavior, but it is important to use them appropriately. Avoid using rewards as bribes or incentives for every little thing, as this can undermine your child's intrinsic motivation. Instead, use rewards as occasional incentives for good behavior or special achievements.

iii) Find ways to show your appreciation

In addition to verbal praise and rewards, there are many other ways to show your appreciation and reinforce positive behavior. These can include gestures of affection, such as hugs or high fives, or small treats or special privileges. By finding ways to show your appreciation, you can make your child feel valued and encourage positive behavior.

By using positive reinforcement, you can help your child feel valued and encourage them to continue exhibiting positive behavior.

2.   Use problem-solving skills

Problem-solving skills are an important aspect of positive parenting. They involve helping your child find solutions to problems on their own, rather than just telling them what to do. By using problem-solving skills, you can help your child develop important critical thinking and decision-making skills and feel more confident and capable.

Here are a few tips for using problem-solving skills:

(i) Ask open-ended questions

Open-ended questions are a great way to encourage your child to think critically and come up with their own solutions. These are questions that cannot be answered with a simple "yes" or "no" response, but instead require more thought and consideration. By asking open-ended questions, you can encourage your child to consider different options and find their own solutions.

(ii) Brainstorm ideas together

Brainstorming is a helpful tool for finding creative solutions to problems. To brainstorm with your child, start by discussing the problem and then generate a list of possible solutions together. Encourage your child to come up with as many ideas as possible, without judgment. This can help your child feel more invested in finding a solution and encourage creative thinking.

(iii) Encourage your child to think critically

Encourage your child to think critically and evaluate the pros and cons of different options. This can help them make informed decisions and find the best solution to the problem.

By using problem-solving skills, you can help your child develop important critical thinking and decision-making skills and feel more confident and capable.

3.   Practice open, honest communication

Open, honest communication is a key aspect of positive parenting. It involves listening to your child's perspective, expressing your own thoughts and feelings, and finding a way to compromise and work together. By having regular, open communication with your child, you can build a strong, supportive relationship and better understand their needs and concerns.

Here are a few tips for practicing open, honest communication:

· Listen actively and empathetically

Active listening involves fully engaging with your child, paying attention to what they are saying, and showing that you understand their perspective. This can involve nodding, making eye contact, and asking open-ended questions. By actively listening to your child, you can show that you value their thoughts and feelings and build a stronger relationship with them.

- Express your own thoughts and feelings

It is also important to express your own thoughts and feelings in a positive, open way. This means being honest and authentic, but also being mindful of your child's feelings. By sharing your own thoughts and feelings, you can model positive communication skills and encourage your child to do the same.

- Find a way to compromise and work together

Open, honest communication also involves finding a way to compromise and work together. This means being open to your child's perspective and finding a solution that works for both of you. By working together, you can strengthen your relationship and find mutually satisfactory solutions.

By practicing open, honest communication with your child, you can build a strong, supportive relationship and better understand their needs and concerns.

4.   Set clear boundaries and expectations

One important aspect of positive parenting is setting clear boundaries and expectations for your child's behavior. Boundaries provide structure and guidance for your child and help them understand what is expected of them. At the same time, it is important to give your child the freedom to make their own decisions and explore their own interests within those boundaries.

Here are a few tips for setting clear boundaries and expectations:

a.   Be specific and consistent

It is important to be specific and consistent when setting boundaries and expectations. This means clearly stating what is and is not acceptable behavior and consistently enforcing those boundaries. This can help your child understand what is expected of them and feel more secure and supported.

b.   Involve your child in the process

Involve your child in the process of setting boundaries and expectations. This can help them feel more invested in following the rules and more aware of their own behavior. You can ask your child for their input, listen to their perspective, and work together to find mutually agreed upon boundaries.

c.   Be flexible and open to negotiation

While it is important to have clear boundaries and expectations, it is also important to be flexible and open to negotiation. This means being willing to adapt and adjust boundaries as your child grows and changes and being open to compromise when appropriate.

By setting clear boundaries and expectations, you can provide structure and guidance for your child while also supporting their independence and autonomy.

Conclusion:

Throughout this book, we have explored the topic of forbearing parents and the importance of finding a balance in parenting style. We have examined the causes of excessive parental control and the effects on children, as well as strategies for overcoming excessive control and implementing positive parenting techniques.

In conclusion, it is important to find a balance in parenting style that provides structure, guidance, and support for children, while also allowing for independence and autonomy. By setting boundaries, encouraging independence and responsibility, and using positive reinforcement and open, honest communication, parents can foster healthy, positive relationships with their children.

It is also important for parents to reflect on their own parenting practices and make changes as needed. This may involve seeking support from trusted sources, such as friends, family, or professionals, or reading up on positive parenting techniques.

We hope that this book has provided valuable insights and strategies for finding a balance in parenting style and fostering healthy, positive relationships with your children. For further reading or resources, we recommend exploring parenting groups, therapy, or books on positive parenting techniques. Thank you for reading.

Made in the USA
Las Vegas, NV
27 December 2024

15444221R00017